A Treasury of
CHILDREN'S SONGS
Forty Favorites to Sing and Play

Music arranged and edited by Dan Fox

THE METROPOLITAN MUSEUM OF ART

HENRY HOLT AND COMPANY
New York

All of the works of art reproduced in this book are from the collections of
The Metropolitan Museum of Art.

FRONT COVER, TITLE PAGE, CONTENTS PAGE: Postcards. Wiener Werkstätte, Austrian, founded 1905.
Color lithographs, 5½ x 3½ inches. Museum Accession.
BACK FLAP: *Monday Morning*. B. J. O. Nordfeldt, American, 1878–1955.
Color woodblock print, 11¾ x 11 in. Gift of Mrs. B. J. O. Nordfeldt, 1955   55.634.79
BACK COVER: *Frog on a Lotus Leaf* (detail). Xiang Shengmou, Chinese, 1597–1658.
From the album *Landscapes, Flowers, and Birds*, ink and color on paper, 11⅛ x 8⅞ in.
Edward Elliott Family Collection, Purchase, The Dillon Fund Gift, 1981   1981.285.3 g

Published by The Metropolitan Museum of Art, New York, and
Henry Holt and Company, LLC, 115 West 18th Street, New York, New York 10011.
Distributed in Canada by H. B. Fenn and Company Ltd.

First Edition
Printed in China
12 11 10 09 08 07 06 05 04 03   5 4 3 2 1

Produced by the Department of Special Publications, The Metropolitan Museum
of Art: Robie Rogge, Publishing Manager; Judith Cressy, Project Editor;
Anna Raff, Designer; Gillian Moran, Production Associate.
All photography by The Metropolitan Museum of Art Photograph Studio unless
otherwise noted.

Visit the Museum's Web site: www.metmuseum.org
Visit Henry Holt's Web site: www.henryholt.com

ISBN 1-58839-017-9 (MMA)
ISBN 0-8050-7445-7 (Holt)

Library of Congress Control Number: 2002116339

Contents

KAISER-
HULDIGUNGS-
FESTZUG
WIEN
1908

GRUPPE 13.
ZEIT KAISER JOSEPH II.
MUSIKANT AUS DEM
ERNTEFEST.

A Note on the Music

In arranging the music for this book, the aim has been simplicity and clarity. All the selections are suitable for beginning to intermediate musicians and each is accompanied by guitar chords. A fingering chart for all of the chords appears at right.

When the piano arrangement is in a key that is awkward for the guitar, capo instructions and alternate chords are given. After the capo is in place, the songs should be played using the chords that appear in parentheses.

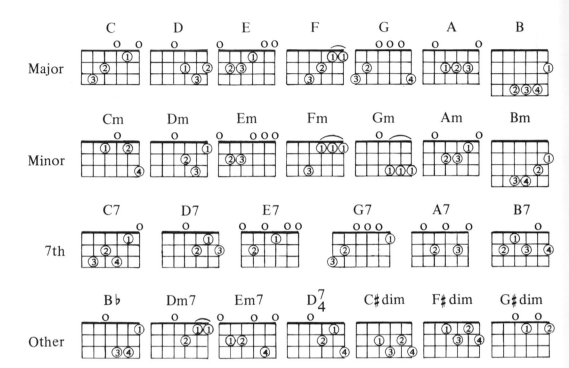

Preface

Gathered together in this book are forty songs of childhood—happy songs and sad songs, songs for young children and songs for older girls and boys. Some are about familiar birds and beasts, others about places and the activities and trades that take place there. The diversity of the songs reflects many of the different kinds of music that children have grown up with over the years.

Our selection is traditional rather than contemporary, everyday rather than seasonal. There are no pop songs or holiday carols. What you will find are examples of each genre of childhood music: nursery songs, ballads, play songs, work songs, spirituals, and folk songs. Some, such as "London Bridge" and "The Mulberry Bush," are songs that children enjoy acting out as well as singing. The music has been arranged and edited by Dan Fox, author of many family songbooks. Each melody is easy to play and suitable for the piano, organ, guitar, violin, or recorder.

All of the songs are paired with works of art from The Metropolitan Museum of Art. The images were chosen to amplify the meaning of every song. It is in the mixture of music and art that the magic of this book lies. It is our hope that this unique presentation will allow songs that have delighted many generations to be experienced afresh.

Amazing Grace

This traditional hymn is about wonder and faith. The words express thankfulness at having survived a time of feeling lost and afraid, and pleasure at the prospect of a life of joy and peace. The painting, *Girl at a Window*, has a spiritual feeling about it, too. The girl seems to be enjoying the wonder of nature in her own peaceful way.

Additional verses:

3.
Through many dangers, toils,
    and snares,
I have already come;
'Tis grace hath brought me safe thus far,
And grace will lead me home.

4.
Yea, when this flesh and heart shall fail
And mortal life shall cease;
I shall possess within the veil
A life of joy and peace.

Girl at a Window
Balthus, French, 1908–2001
Oil on canvas, 63 x 63¾ in., 1957

Moderately

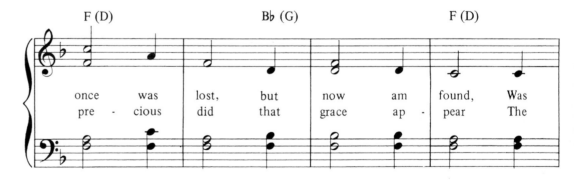

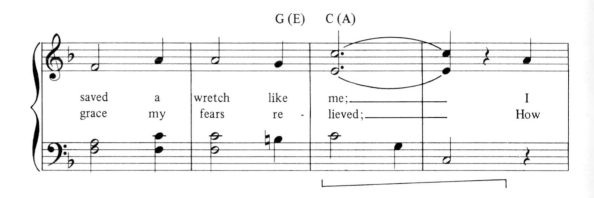

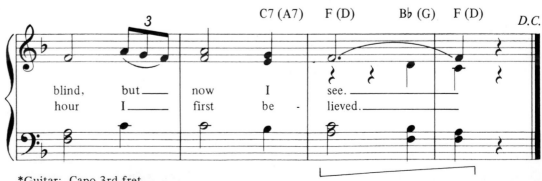

*Guitar: Capo 3rd fret

Allegretto

Baa, baa, black sheep, have you an-y wool?

mp

Baa, Baa, Black Sheep

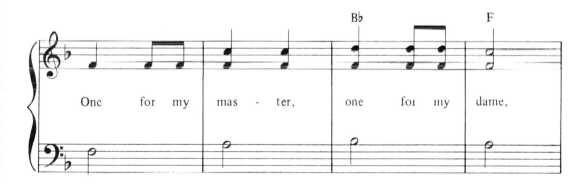

Yes, sir, yes, sir, three bags full.

For more than two hundred years, "Baa, Baa, Black Sheep" has been a favorite nursery rhyme in Britain and the United States. The tune, however, may have come from France, where it is sung with different words. Some breeds of sheep yield more wool than others, and the sheep in this song has enough for three people.

One for my mas-ter, one for my dame,

One for the lit-tle boy who lives down the lane.

Needlework picture
Keturah Rawlins, American, ca. 1740
Wool and silk on linen, 16¾ x 17½ in.

9

Billy Boy

It is not hard to imagine the affectionate young man in *The Music Lesson* as "charming Billy," visiting his wife-to-be at her mother's house. As this song is known today, it is playful and teasing, but the tune and some of the words come from a much older English ballad, "Lord Randal." In it, Lord Randal is poisoned by his lover.

Not fast (♩ = 1 beat)

1. Oh,_____ where have you been, Bil - ly
2. Did she bid you to come in, Bil - ly

mp

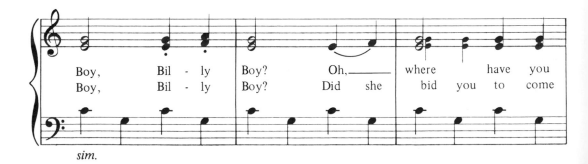

Boy, Bil - ly Boy? Oh,_____ where have you
Boy, Bil - ly Boy? Did she bid you to come

sim.

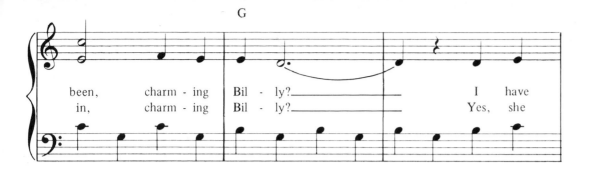

been,   charm - ing | Bil - ly?_____ | I   have
in,   charm - ing | Bil - ly?_____ | Yes, she

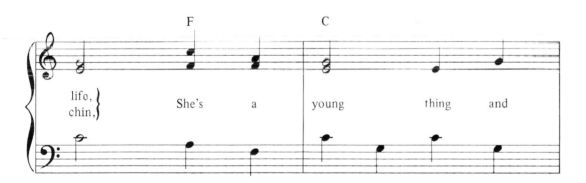

been to   seek a | wife, She's the | dar - ling of   my
bade me   to   come | in,   There's a | dim - ple on   her

lifo, }   She's   a   young   thing   and
chin, }

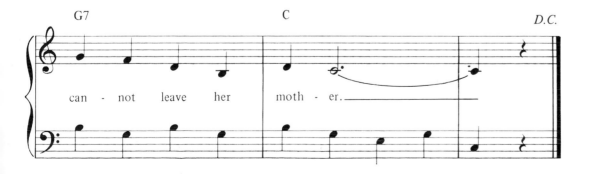

can - not leave her | moth - er._____ |

Additional verses:

3.

Can she bake a cherry pie, Billy Boy,
    Billy Boy?
Can she bake a cherry pie,
    charming Billy?
She can bake a cherry pie
In the twinkling of an eye,
She's a young thing and cannot leave
    her mother.

4.

How old is she, Billy Boy, Billy Boy?
How old is she, charming Billy?
She's three times six, four times seven,
Twenty-eight and eleven,
She's a young thing and cannot leave
    her mother.

The Music Lesson (detail)
John George Brown, American, 1831–1913
Oil on canvas, 24 x 20 in., 1870

Bingo

No one knows what kind of dog Bingo really was. The dog at right is a special breed of beagle and was painted from life by Rosa Bonheur, famous as a painter of animals. She tried to get an exact likeness of this handsome dog, whose alert expression and tense pose suggest that he might be following the scent of a trail.

Brightly (♩ = 1 beat)

There was a farm-er who had a dog, And Bing-o was his

name - o. B - I - N - G - O,

B - I - N - G - O, B - I -

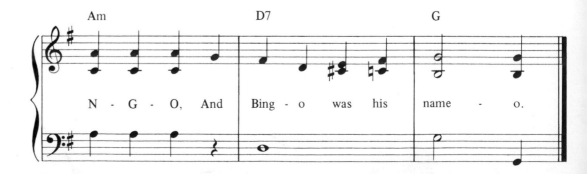

N - G - O, And Bing-o was his name - o.

A Limier Briquet Hound (detail)
Rosa Bonheur, French, 1822–1899
Oil on canvas, 14½ x 18 in., ca. 1880

Clementine

The men in Winslow Homer's *Camp Fire*, painted in 1880, may well have known the sad story of Clementine. By then the Gold Rush and the forty-niners had become part of American folklore. Although Clementine and her father come to an unhappy end, it's hard not to smile at the comical touches like the "herring boxes without topses."

Moderately   F (D)*

1. In a cav - ern, in a can - yon, Ex - ca -
2. Light she was and like a fair - y, And her

mp

C7 (A7)

vat - ing for a mine, Lived a min - er, for - ty -
shoes were num - ber nine; Her - ring box - es with - out

*Guitar: Capo 3rd fret

14

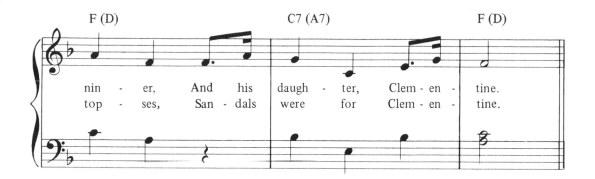

nin - er, And his | daugh - ter, Clem - en - tine.
top - ses, San - dals were for Clem - en - tine.

Additional verses:

3.
Drove she ducklings to the water,
Ev'ry morning just at nine;
Hit her foot against a splinter,
Fell into the foaming brine.
(Chorus)

4.
Ruby lips above the water,
Blowing bubbles soft and fine;
But alas, he was no swimmer,
So he lost his Clementine.
(Chorus)

5.
Then the miner, forty-niner,
Soon began to peak and pine;
Thought he oughter join his daughter,
Now he's with his Clementine.
(Chorus)

Chorus F (D)

Oh my dar - ling, Oh my dar - ling, Oh my

mf

C7 (A7)

dar - ling, Clem - en - tine, You are lost and gone for -

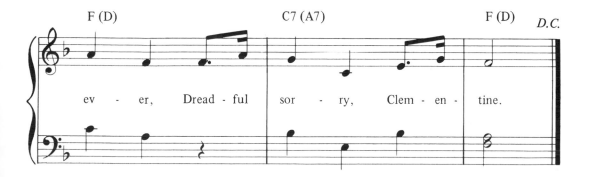

F (D) C7 (A7) F (D) *D.C.*

ev - er, Dread - ful sor - ry, Clem - en - tine.

Camp Fire (detail)
Winslow Homer, American, 1836–1910
Oil on canvas, 23¾ x 38⅛ in., 1880

15

Did You Ever See a Lassie?

Did You Ever See a Lassie" is a very old song, and the tune comes from an even older folk ditty. Traditionally, girls would hold out their skirts, as in this picture, first this way, then that way, when singing the song.

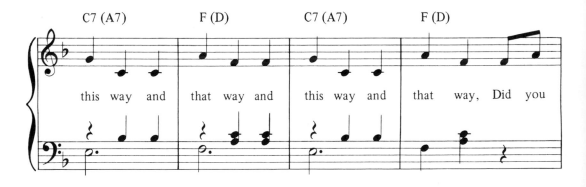

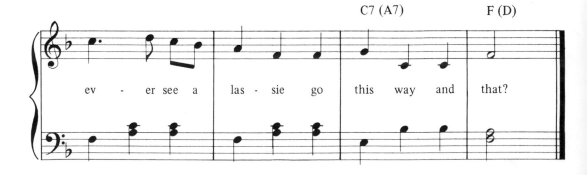

Down by the Riverside

A river flows very gently in this painting by Asher B. Durand. Its setting of pasturelands and shade trees is a scene of perfect harmony, an ideal expressed in the words of this song, which tells of a longing for peace and rest after the struggles of life.

Moderately, with a strong beat

1. Gon - na   lay down   my   sword and shield,
2. Gon - na   meet my   Lord   Je - sus,
3. Gon - na   lay down   my   bur - den,

Down by the

riv - er - side,___   Down by   the   riv - er - side,___

Down by the riv - er - side,—

{ Gon - na lay down my
{ Gon - na meet my Lord
{ Gon - na lay down my

{ sword and shield,)
{ Je - sus,)
{ bur - den,)

Down by the riv - er - side,— Gon - na

Perhaps the most moving folk songs ever to come from America are spirituals like "Down by the Riverside," sung by African-Americans in the South, in the days of slavery. The words, usually based on stories or phrases from the Bible, evoked feelings and memories all could share, and the rhythms of the chorus were often stressed by clapping hands.

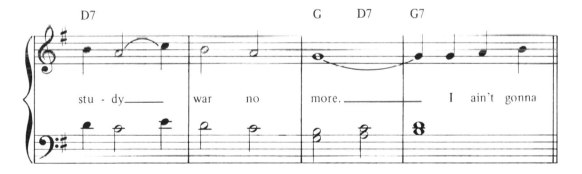

stu - dy____ war no more.____ I ain't gonna

Chorus

stu - dy war no more, I ain't gonna stu - dy war no

Summer Afternoon (detail)
Asher B. Durand, American, 1796–1886
Oil on canvas, 22½ x 35 in., 1865

(continued on next page)

19

Down by the Riverside

In the nineteenth century, John F. Kensett was one of America's foremost painters of the Hudson River School and was renowned for his views of nature and water. When Kensett's painting at right first entered the Metropolitan Museum's collection, it was titled *River Scene*. Later, it was retitled *Summer Day on Conesus Lake*. But whether river or lake, it expresses the peaceful calm of a lazy summer afternoon.

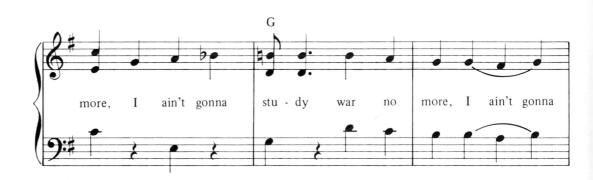

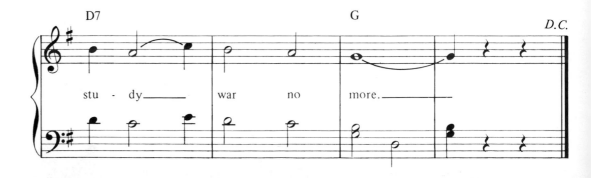

Summer Day on Conesus Lake (detail)
John F. Kensett, American, 1816–1872
Oil on canvas, 24⅛ x 36⅜ in., 1870

Moderately

Down by the sta-tion ear-ly in the morn-ing,

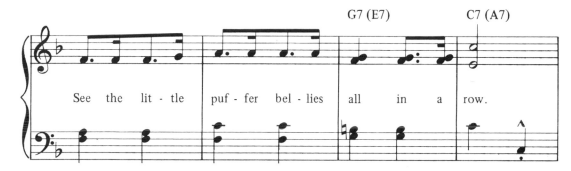

See the lit-tle puf-fer bel-lies all in a row.

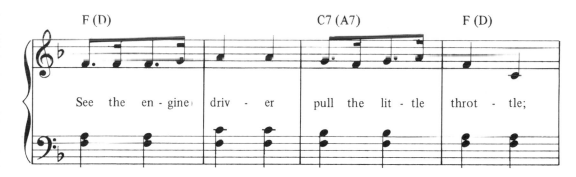

See the en-gine driv-er pull the lit-tle throt-tle;

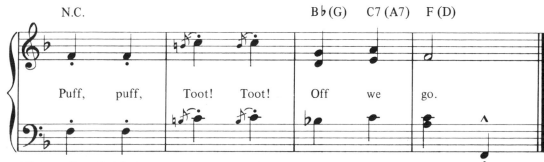

Puff, puff, Toot! Toot! Off we go.

*Guitar: Capo 3rd fret

Down by the Station

People were so thrilled by the invention of the steam loco-motive early in the nineteenth century that they soon began to make up songs and stories about railroads and railroad workers. The second steam locomotive invented by the British engineer George Stephenson was called "Puffing Billy," and it may have been the origin of the "puffer bellies" mentioned in this song.

Grand Central Station (detail)
Colin Campbell Cooper, American, 1856–1937
Oil on canvas, 33 x 44¾ in., 1909

Eensy Weensy Spider

Some people are afraid of all spiders, but they need not be. Most spiders are not dangerous to people and are actually helpful. They use their delicate-looking but surprisingly strong webs to catch many insects. Spiders are fascinating to watch and are more persevering than many human beings. The tiny spider in this song may be washed down the waterspout by the rain, but as soon as the sun comes out, he climbs back again.

Like a slow march

The een-sy ween-sy spi-der went up the wa-ter-spout.

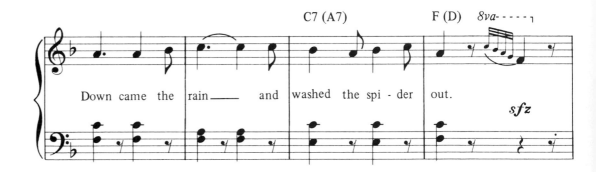

Down came the rain____ and washed the spi-der out.

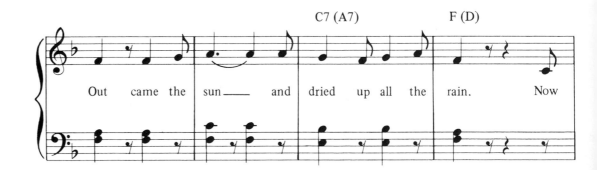

Out came the sun____ and dried up all the rain. Now

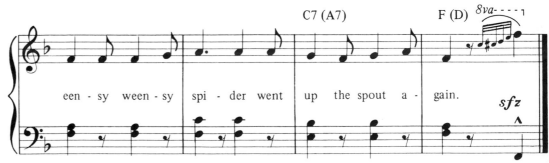

een-sy ween-sy spi-der went up the spout a-gain.

*Guitar: Capo 3rd fret

Spider (detail)
Taki Katei, Japanese, 1830–1901
Leaf from the album *Flowers and Birds*, ink and color on silk, 10 x 12 in.

Janitor's Holiday
Paul Sample, American, 1896–1974
Oil on canvas, 26 x 40 in., 1936

Like a march

F (D)*

1. The farm - er in the dell,_____ The
2. The farm - er takes a wife,_____ The

mf

farm - er in the dell,_____ Heigh - ho, the
farm - er takes a wife,_____ Heigh - ho, the

Dm (Bm)   F (D)   C7 (A7)   F (D)   *D.C.*

der - ry - o, The farm - er in the dell._____
der - ry - o, The farm - er takes a wife._____

*Guitar: Capo 3rd fret

The Farmer in the Dell

In this painting by Paul Sample, the little farm, with its traditional red barn, is surrounded by hills, as suggested by the song's "dell," or small valley. Everything on this farm looks as neat as a pin, although no one seems to be working very hard.

Additional verses:

3.
The wife takes a child, *etc.*
4.
The child takes a nurse, *etc.*
5.
The nurse takes a dog, *etc.*
6.
The dog takes a cat, *etc.*
7.
The cat takes a rat, *etc.*
8.
The rat takes the cheese, *etc.*
9.
The cheese stands alone, *etc.*

A Frog Went A-Courtin'

The Chinese artist who painted this frog on a lotus leaf did so with great sensitivity, for to Chinese and Japanese artists, a bird on a twig or a beetle on a blade of grass is just as interesting a subject as something grand, like a mountain. This frog crouching on his leaf among the rushes looks as if he could leap off at any moment.

Frog on a Lotus Leaf
Xiang Shengmou, Chinese, 1597–1658
From the album *Landscapes, Flowers, and Birds*,
ink and color on paper, 11⅛ x 8⅞ in., 1639

*Guitar: Capo 3rd fret

Additional verses:

3.

"Yes, Sir Frog, I sit and spin." (hum)
"Yes, Sir Frog I sit and spin,
Please Mr. Froggie, won't you come
    in?" (hum)

4.

The froggie said, "My dear, I've come
    to see," (hum)
The froggie said, "My dear, I've come
    to see
If you, Miss Mousie, will marry me,"
    (hum)

5.

"Oh, yes, Sir Frog, I'll marry you."
    (hum)
"Oh yes, Sir Frog, I'll marry you,
And we'll have children two by two,"
    (hum)

6.

The frog and mouse they went to
    France. (hum)
The frog and mouse they went to
    France,
And that's the end of my romance.
    (hum)

Brightly, with spirit

F (D)*   C7 (A7)

mf

Go in and out the win - dow, Go

Go In and Out the Window

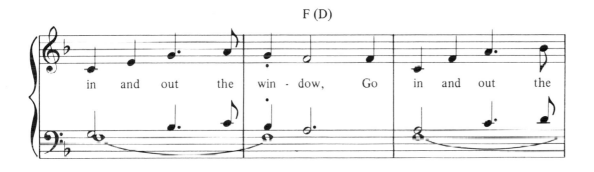

F (D)

in and out the win - dow, Go in and out the

In this sunny image by Franz Melchers, the wide-open windows draw the imagination indoors and out. The song is an old favorite, and children enjoy inventing additional verses such as "Go round and round the village," "Stand and face your partner," and "Go up and down the staircase."

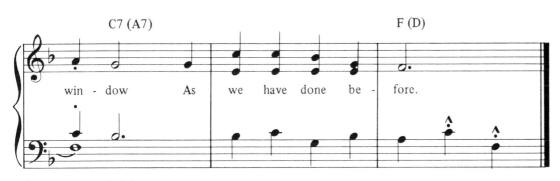

C7 (A7)   F (D)

win - dow As we have done be - fore.

*Guitar: Capo 3rd fret

Summer
Franz M. Melchers, Belgian, 1868–1944
Hand-tinted lithograph illustration from *L'An*
(poems by Thomas Braun), published in Brussels by
E. Lyon-Claesen, 9¹⁵⁄₁₆ x 9¹⁵⁄₁₆ in., 1897

Greensleeves

"Greensleeves" was a favorite song in the days of England's great Queen Elizabeth I, and Shakespeare mentioned the song in one of his plays. It is a melancholy tune and the words are sad, for the singer complains that although he and his lady were once friends and he gave her beautiful presents, she no longer cares for him. Even so, he still loves her and hopes she will come back to him.

Moderately flowing

1. A- las, my love,____ you do me wrong____ to
2. I have been read- y at your hand____ to

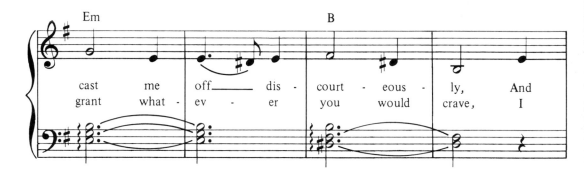

cast me off____ dis- court- eous- ly, And
grant what- ev- er you would crave, I

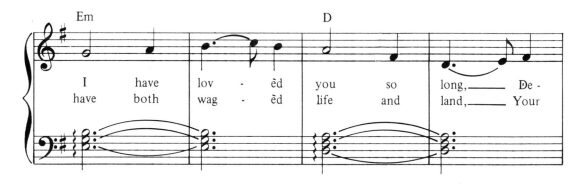

I have lov- ĕd you so long,____ De-
have both wag- ĕd life and land,____ Your

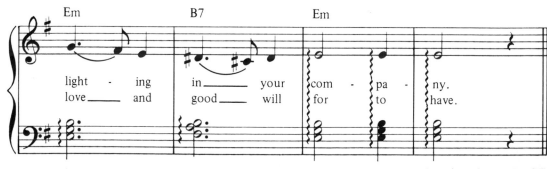

light- ing in____ your com- pa- ny.
love____ and good____ will for to have.

Mezzetin (detail)
Jean Antoine Watteau, French, 1684–1721
Oil on canvas, 21¾ x 17 in., probably 1718–20

(continued on page 35)

Greensleeves

Green - sleeves____ was all my joy,____

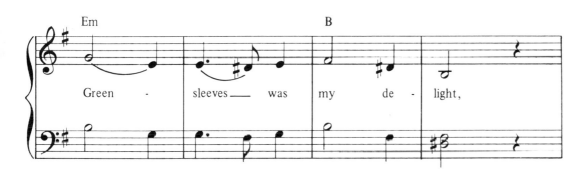

Green - sleeves____ was my de - light,

Green - sleeves,____ my heart of gold,____ And

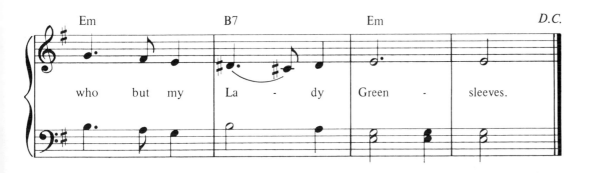

who but my La - dy Green - sleeves.

Imagine looking out your window and spying an eighteenth-century musician seated in your backyard singing a song. The American artist Jane Freilicher painted this intriguing contemporary scene, which places the musician inside as well as out, inspired by Jean Watteau's eighteenth-century painting on the previous page.

The Lute Player
Jane Freilicher, American, b. 1924
Oil on canvas, 36 x 36 in., 1993

Hickory, Dickory, Dock

It's not certain that anyone has actually ever seen mice running to the top of a clock and then back down again. If any mice could do it, however, these engaging little rodents from a Japanese scroll look like sure candidates.

ABOVE AND BELOW: *Mice* (details)
Kyōsai (Kawanabe Shūsaburo), Japanese, 1831–1889
Handscroll, ink and wash on paper,
10⅞ in. x 20 ft. 8 in.

Moderately (♩. = 1 beat)

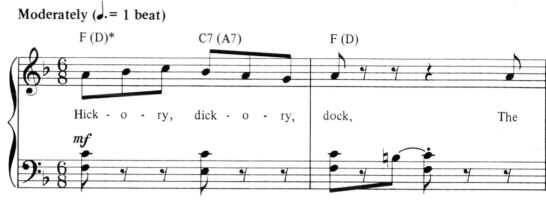

Hick - o - ry, dick - o - ry, dock, The mouse ran up the clock. The clock struck one, A-

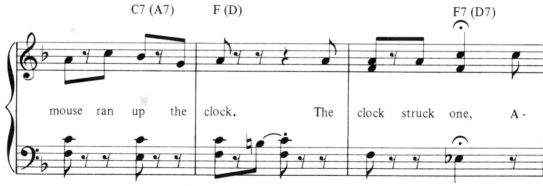

way he run! Hick - o - ry, dick - o - ry, dock.

*Guitar: Capo 3rd fret

Home on the Range

Americans have always been drawn to wide open spaces, and from pioneer days to the present, the West has had a special appeal. *Steers at Play* captures that appeal playfully in a scene complete with a cowboy, snow-capped mountains, and grazing land, and a sky that's "not cloudy all day."

Moderately

Oh, give me a home where the buf - fa - lo roam, Where the

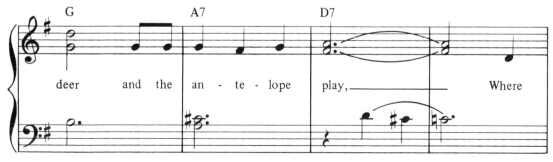

deer and the an - te - lope play,_____ Where

Steers at Play
Lawrence H. Lebduska, American, 1894–1966
Oil on canvas, 25 x 30 in., 1937

(continued on next page)

Home on the Range

In the foreground of this monumental view of the Rocky Mountains, Albert Bierstadt painted a Shoshone Indian camp. Bierstadt used both photography and sketches to record the scenes he witnessed.

ABOVE AND DETAIL AT RIGHT: *The Rocky Mountains, Lander's Peak*
Albert Bierstadt, American, 1830–1902
Oil on canvas, 6 ft. 1½ in. x 10 ft. ¾ in., 1863

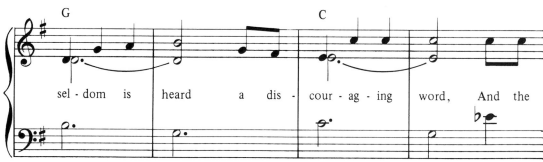

sel - dom is heard a dis - cour - ag - ing word, And the

skies are not cloud - y all day.

Chorus

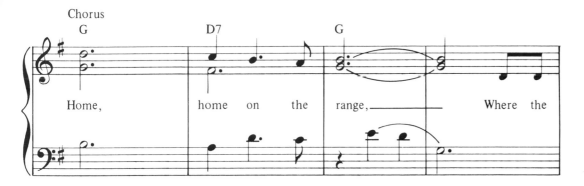

Home, home on the range,___ Where the

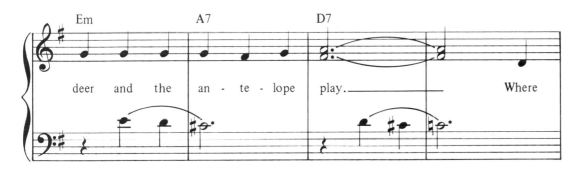

deer and the an - te - lope play.___ Where

sel - dom is heard a dis - cour - ag - ing word, And the

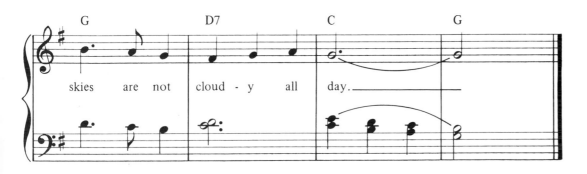

skies are not cloud - y all day.___

Not too fast, with a lilt

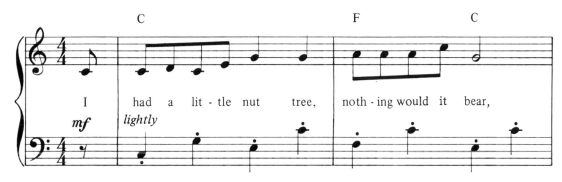

I had a lit-tle nut tree, noth-ing would it bear,

mf lightly

I Had a Little Nut Tree

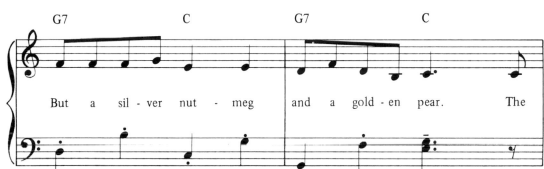

But a sil-ver nut-meg and a gold-en pear. The

Some people think that this song, with its soft, gentle melody, refers to a visit by Juana of Castile, daughter of King Ferdinand V of Spain, to the English court in 1506. But the words of the song make the event seem like a fairy tale, for only a magical tree could bear a silver nutmeg and a golden pear. Little trees bearing enormous fruit were a familiar motif in seventeenth-century needlework, such as the one shown here.

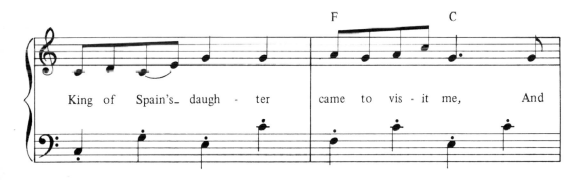

King of Spain's daugh-ter came to vis-it me, And

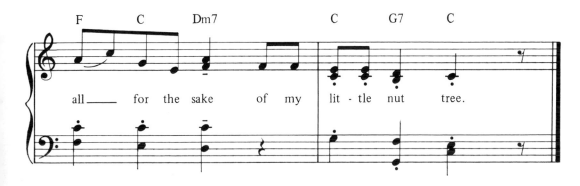

all ____ for the sake of my lit-tle nut tree.

Esther and Ahasuerus (detail)
English, mid-17th century
Colored silk embroidered
on canvas, 16½ x 20¼ in.

41

I Love Little Pussy

Although children love kittens and puppies, they sometimes play with them too roughly. This rhyme is a reminder that if you treat pets kindly and gently, they will be loving companions. The sleeping kitten in this painting seems very relaxed and content.

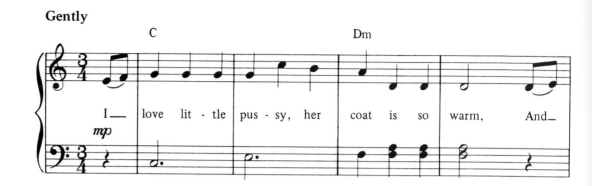

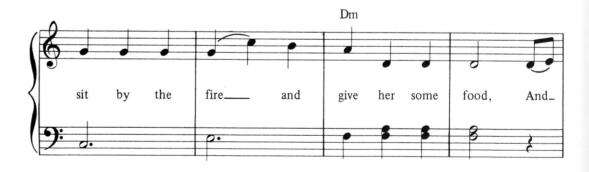

Spring Play in a Tang Garden (detail)
Chinese, 18th century
Handscroll, color on silk, 1 ft. 2¾ in. x 8 ft. 8 in.

It's Raining, It's Pouring

Wistfully

It's rain - ing, it's pour - ing, The

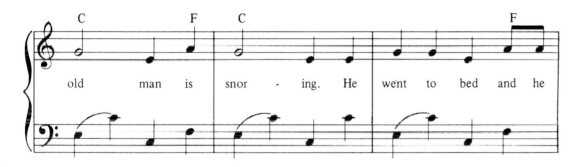

old man is snor - ing. He went to bed and he

bumped his head, And he would-n't get up in the morn - ing.

Using very few colors, the Japanese artist Utagawa Hiroshige was able to capture the atmosphere of a sudden rainstorm. To protect themselves, some of the people scurrying across the bridge huddle under paper umbrellas. While the old man in the song keeps warm and dry snoring in bed, these people probably wish that the rain would go away.

Sudden Shower on the Great Bridge (detail)
Utagawa Hiroshige, Japanese, 1797–1858
From *One Hundred Views of Edo*,
polychrome woodblock print, 13⅜ x 9½ in., 1857

I've Been Working on the Railroad

Railroads have played such an important part in the expansion of the United States, and especially in the opening of the West, that it is no wonder they have inspired so many folk songs and works of art. This popular song captures the robust spirit of the early builders of the railways.

Like a slow march

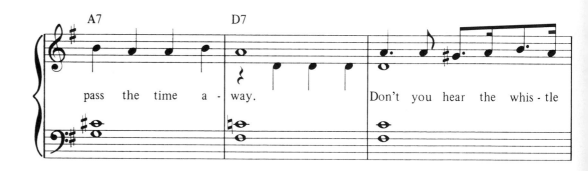

Railroad Crossing, the Berkshires (detail)
George Luks, American, 1866–1933
Watercolor and pencil on paper,
13⅞ x 19⅞ in.

(continued on page 48)

I've Been Working on the Railroad

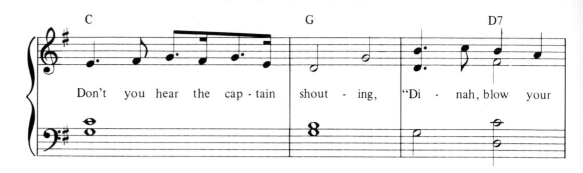

Don't you hear the cap-tain shout-ing, "Di - nah, blow your

horn?"   Di - nah, won't you blow,

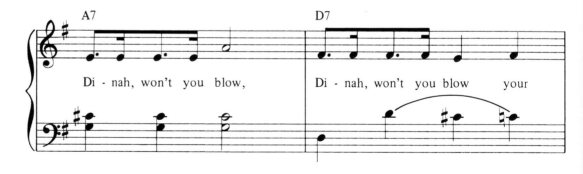

Di - nah, won't you blow,   Di - nah, won't you blow   your

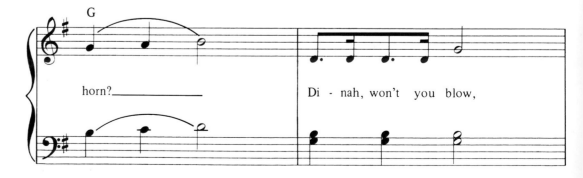

horn?____   Di - nah, won't you blow,

Hudson River Railroad Station, with a View of Manhattan College (detail)
American, 19th century
Watercolor and ink on off-white wove paper,
22½ x 35½ in.

48

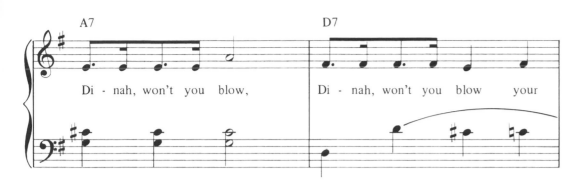

Di - nah, won't you blow, Di - nah, won't you blow your

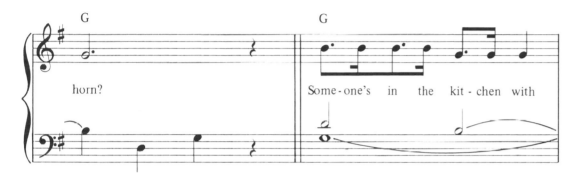

horn? Some - one's in the kit - chen with

Di - nah, Some - one's in the kit - chen, I

know, _____ Some - one's in the kit - chen with

(continued on next page)

Route of the Black Diamond (detail)
Mark Baum, American, 1903–1997
Oil on canvas, 22¼ x 30⅛ in., ca. 1940

49

I've Been Working on the Railroad

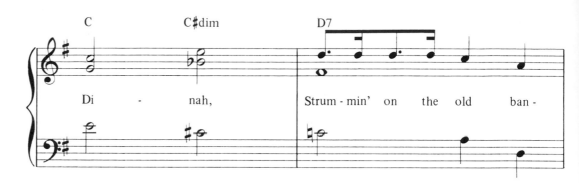

Di - nah, Strum - min' on the old ban -

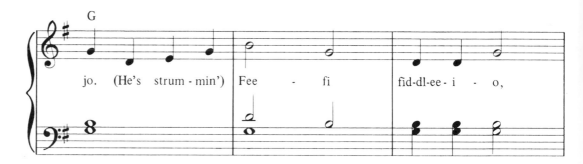

jo. (He's strum - min') Fee - fi fid-dl-ee - i - o,

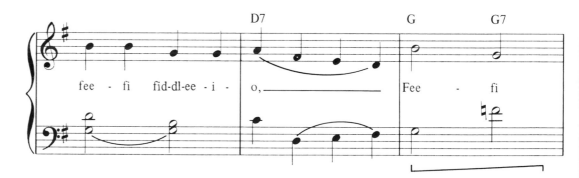

fee - fi fid-dl-ee - i - o, _____ Fee - fi

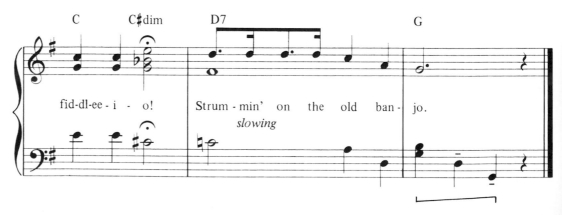

fid-dl-ee - i - o! Strum - min' on the old ban - jo.
slowing

The 9:45 Accommodation (detail)
Edward Lamson Henry, American, 1841–1919
Oil on canvas, 16 x 30⅝ in., 1867

Jack and Jill

In some collections of nursery rhymes published in the nineteenth century, the story of Jack and Jill and their misadventure was extended to fifteen verses, but usually only the two included here are sung.

Moderately (♪.= 1 beat)

1. Jack and Jill went up the hill, To
2. Up Jack got and home he ran, As

mp

fetch a pail of wa - ter. Jack fell down and
fast as he could ca - per. There his moth - er

broke his crown, And Jill came tum - bling af - ter.
bound his head, With vin - e - gar and brown pa - per.

Jack and Jill
Went up the hill,
To fetch a pail of water;
Jack fell down
And broke his crown,
And Jill came tumbling after.

TOP: *Children of the Empire*
Valerie Grienauer, Austrian, active 1920s
Stencil-colored linocut

ABOVE: *Jack and Jill*
Kate Greenaway, British, 1846–1901
Illustration from *Mother Goose or the Old Nursery Rhymes*, George Routledge and Sons, London and New York

Lavender's Blue

There's a "let's pretend" feeling to this nursery song. Words like "dilly dilly" make no sense, and lavender is never green, but the words are enjoyable in the rhyme. The playmates imagine themselves growing up to be king and queen.

Rather quickly

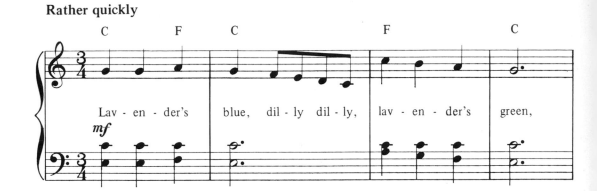

Lav - en - der's blue, dil - ly dil - ly, lav - en - der's green,

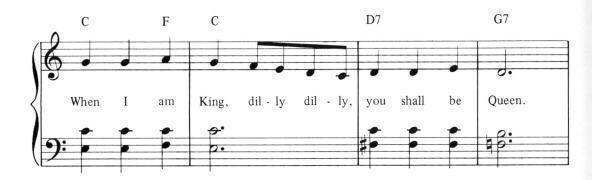

When I am King, dil - ly dil - ly, you shall be Queen.

Who told you so, dil - ly dil - ly, who told you so?

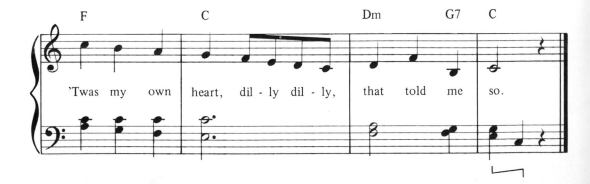

'Twas my own heart, dil - ly dil - ly, that told me so.

Flowers of the Field (detail)
Luis F. Mora, American, 1874–1940
Oil on canvas, 40 x 36 in., 1913

52

Briskly (♩. = 1 beat)

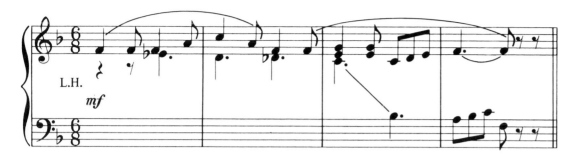

Lazy Mary

Getting up in the morning is never easy, and this song may have started in England as a game, with one or more children being "mother" and another child or children playing "Mary" and pretending to be fast asleep. Perhaps the pretty young shepherdess in this picture by the French painter François Boucher will not mind being awakened when she sees the handsome young shepherd who is tickling her neck.

F (D)* C7 (A7)

1. La - zy Mar - y, will you get up, Will you get up, will
2. Oh, no, moth-er, I won't get up, I won't get up, I

F (D)

you get up? La - zy Mar - y, will you get up, Will
won't get up! Oh, no, moth - er, I won't get up, I

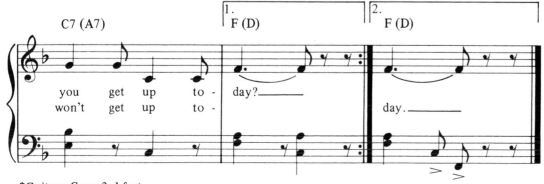

C7 (A7) 1. F (D) 2. F (D)

you get up to - day?_____
won't get up to - day._____

The Interrupted Sleep (detail)
François Boucher, French, 1703–1770
Oil on canvas, 32¼ x 29⅝ in., 1750

*Guitar: Capo 3rd fret

London Bridge

England's London Bridge, over the River Thames, has a long history. The first one was made of wood, but in the Middle Ages it was replaced by a stone bridge with houses and a chapel on it. This bridge was often damaged by fire, and in 1831, when it was almost ready to fall down, it was replaced by a new bridge (shown at right), which was also pulled down and replaced by a modern bridge in 1971.

Moderately

1. Lon - don Bridge is fall - ing down, Fall - ing down, fall - ing down,
2. Build it up with gold and sil - ver, Gold and sil - ver, gold and sil - ver,

Lon - don Bridge is fall - ing down, My fair la - dy.
Build it up with gold and sil - ver, My fair la - dy.

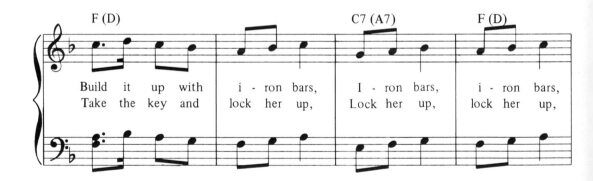

Build it up with i - ron bars, I - ron bars, i - ron bars,
Take the key and lock her up, Lock her up, lock her up,

Build it up with i - ron bars, My fair la - dy.
Take the key and lock her up, My fair la - dy.

New London Bridge (detail)
Thomas Sidney Cooper, British, 1803–1902
Hand-colored lithograph, 7¾ x 14½ in., 1831

* Guitar: Capo 3rd fret

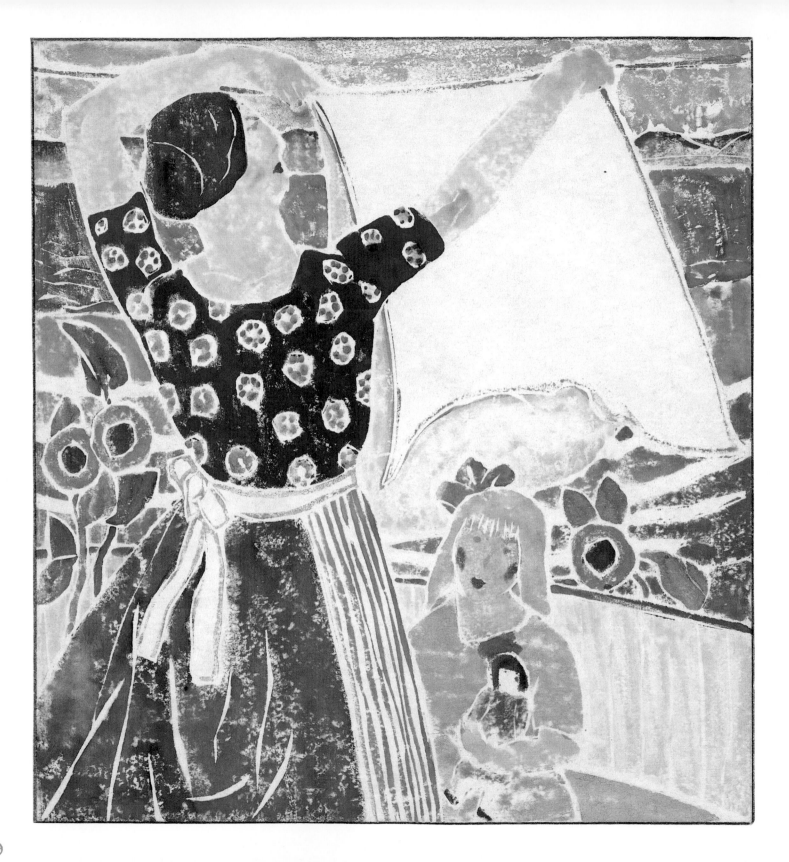

Quickly (♩. = 1 beat)

The Mulberry Bush

Long before the days of washing machines and electricity, laundry was done by hand and hung outdoors on clotheslines to dry in the sun and wind. Monday, by tradition, was laundry day in many households, as is noted in the title of this colorful woodblock print.

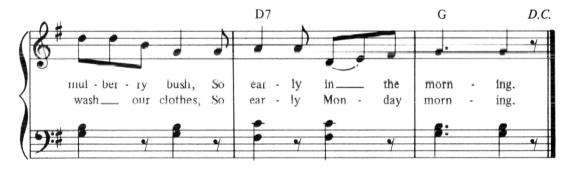

Monday Morning
B. J. O. Nordfeldt, American, 1878–1955
Color woodblock print, 11¾ x 11 in.

Additional verses:

3.
This is the way we iron our clothes, *etc.*
So early Tuesday morning.

4.
This is the way we scrub the floor, *etc.*
So early Wednesday morning.

5.
This is the way we mend our clothes, *etc.*
So early Thursday morning.

6.
This is the way we sweep the house, *etc.*
So early Friday morning.

7.
This is the way we bake our bread, *etc.*
So early Saturday morning.

8.
This is the way we go to church, *etc.*
So early Sunday morning.

My Bonnie Lies Over the Ocean

Moderately fast

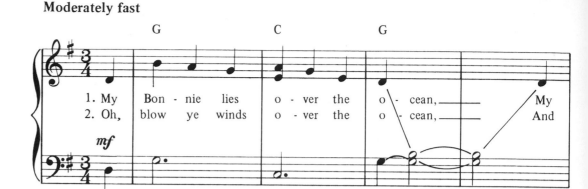

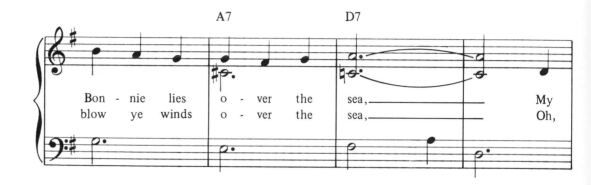

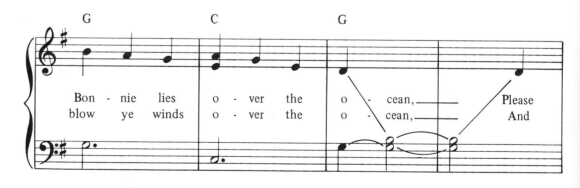

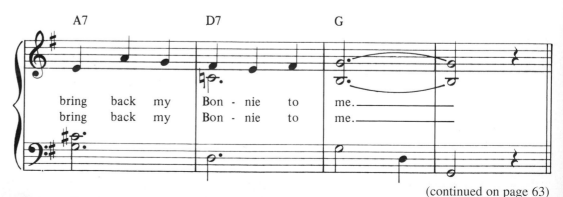

Nearly everyone has dreamed of crossing the ocean to far-away places. Often after a long journey a sailor becomes homesick, while those back home look forward to their loved one's return. Winslow Homer, who lived in Maine, painted many of his most famous watercolors far from home, off the islands of the Bahamas.

Sloop, Nassau (detail)
Winslow Homer, American, 1836–1910
Watercolor and graphite on off-white wove paper,
14⅞ x 21⅜ in.

(continued on page 63)

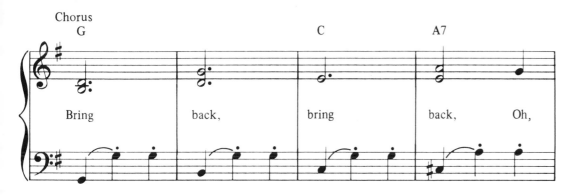

Chorus

G		C	A7
Bring	back,	bring	back, Oh,

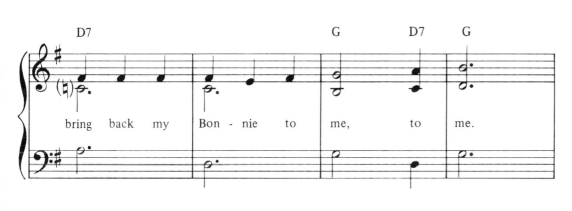

D7		G	D7	G
bring back my	Bon - nie to	me,	to	me.

My Bonnie Lies Over the Ocean

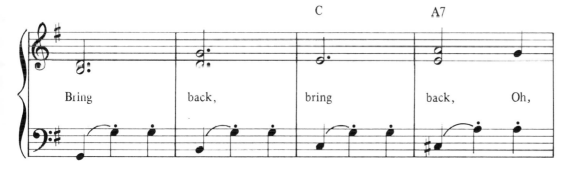

		C	A7
Bring	back,	bring	back, Oh,

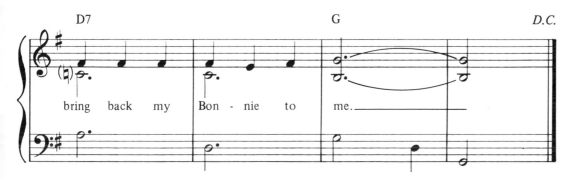

D7		G	D.C.
bring back my	Bon - nie to	me._____	

ABOVE: Postcard
Oskar Kokoschka, Austrian, 1886–1980,
produced by the Wiener Werkstätte, Austrian,
founded 1905
Color lithograph, 3½ x 5½ in.

LEFT: *West Point (Casco Bay), Maine* (detail)
John Marin, American, 1870–1953
Watercolor on paper, 14⅛ x 16⅜ in., 1914

Oats, Peas, and Beans

This song has the vigorous rhythm of a folk dance, and it's hard not to keep time by clapping your hands when the song is sung. The American artist Yvonne Jacquette painted the accompanying aerial view of a farm in southern Maine after making sketches of the farm from a single-engine plane.

Moderately (♩.= 1 beat)

bar - ley grow, Can you or I or an - y - one know How
part - ner,____ O - pen the ring and bring____ one in While
la la la,____ Tra la la la la____ la la, Tra

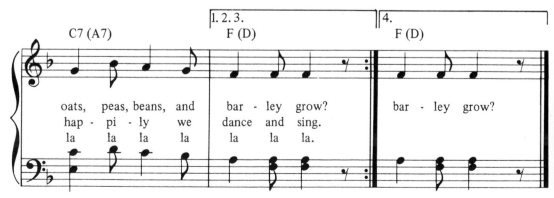

oats, peas, beans, and bar - ley grow?   bar - ley grow?
hap - pi - ly we   dance and sing.
la la la la   la la la.

*Guitar: Capo 3rd fret

Gently flowing

Oh, how love-ly is the eve-ning,

p

Oh, How Lovely Is the Evening

is the eve-ning, When the bells are

This song and the softly lit painting evoke the magical mood of evening, when the light is fading and the world is seen in silhouette. The song is a round, to be sung by several people, with each voice entering in turn, overlapping the preceding voice, then going back to the beginning on reaching the end. The ding-dong refrain of the church bells makes this round especially effective.

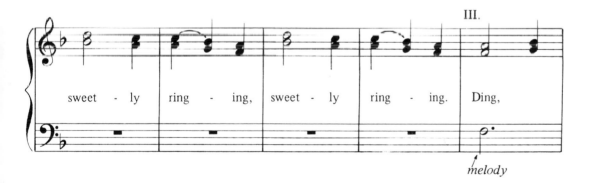

sweet-ly ring-ing, sweet-ly ring-ing. Ding,

melody

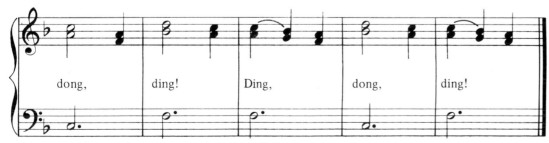

dong, ding! Ding, dong, ding!

To complete the round, sing or play the left hand alone at **III.**

Oh! Susanna

This happy-go-lucky song was popular all over America. Written by Stephen Foster, it quickly became the anthem of the Gold Rush. The song has the jolly feeling of someone setting out on the open road singing and strumming on a banjo or guitar. Philadelphia artist Thomas Eakins spent some time sketching and photographing the American West, but painted this portrait of a banjo-playing cowboy back in his Philadelphia studio.

Cowboy Singing (detail)
Thomas Eakins, American, 1844–1916
Watercolor and graphite on off-white wove paper,
18⅞ x 14¹⁵⁄₁₆ in., ca. 1892

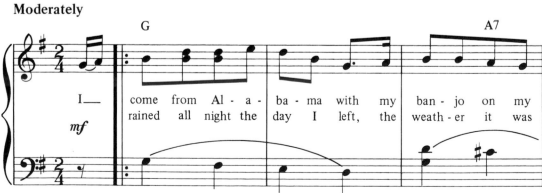

Moderately

I— come from Al - a - ba - ma with my ban - jo on my
rained all night the day I left, the weath - er it was

knee, I'm goin' to Lou-'si-an-a, my_____
dry, The_ sun so hot I froze to death, Su-

true love for to see. It_
san-na don't you cry.___

Chorus

Oh! Su-san-na, Oh, don't you cry for me. I've_

come from Al-a-ba-ma with my ban-jo on my knee.__

Old MacDonald

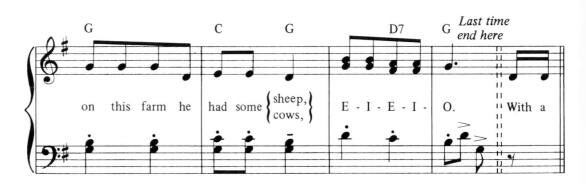

Children love to imitate animal sounds, and this song gives them a chance to moo like a cow, quack like a duck, and so on. The peaceful setting of the Vermont farm in the painting at right would be an ideal spot to hear those animal voices.

Old Mac-Don-ald had a farm, E - I - E - I - O. And on this farm he had some { sheep, cows, } E - I - E - I - O. With a

Last time end here

1. baa - baa here and a baa - baa there,
2. moo - moo here and a moo - moo there,

Repeat as necessary, then D.C.

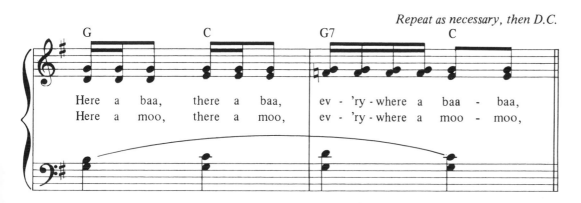

Here a baa, there a baa, ev - 'ry - where a baa - baa,
Here a moo, there a moo, ev - 'ry - where a moo - moo,

ABOVE: *Heifers, Pawlet, Vermont*
Altoon Sultan, American, b. 1948
Oil on canvas, 30 x 72 in., 1987

LEFT: *Chookyard (detail)*
William Robinson, Australian, b. 1936
Charcoal and pastel on paper, 22¼ x 30 in.,
ca. 1983–84

71

On Top of Old Smokey

In this song, the singer recalls a time when he and the one he loved walked together on a snowy mountain. Now he feels that if he had been less timid, she would never have left him for someone else and made him so unhappy. This painting by Jerome Thompson shares the tender, wistful mood of the song.

Rather quickly

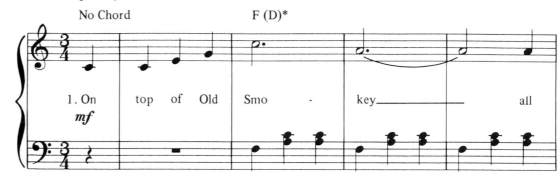

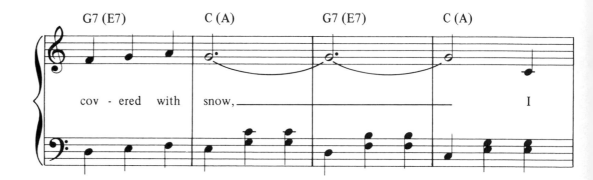

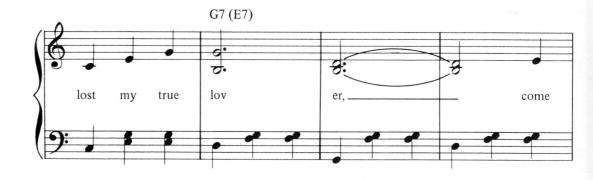

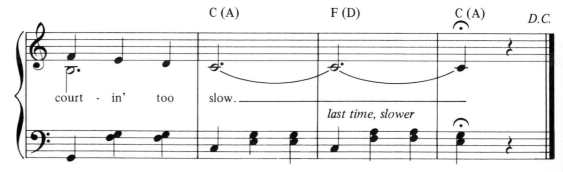

The Belated Party on Mansfield Mountain
Jerome B. Thompson, American, 1814–1886
Oil on canvas, 38 x 63⅛ in., 1858

*Guitar: Capo 3rd fret

72

Additional verses:

2.
For courtin's a pleasure, but parting is grief,
And a falsehearted lover is worse than a thief.

3.
For a thief, he will rob you and take what you have,
But a falsehearted lover will send you to your grave.

4.
She'll (he'll) hug you and kiss you and tell you more lies
Than the crossties on the railroad or the stars in the skies.

5.
Repeat first verse.

Pop! Goes the Weasel

The thought of a mischievous monkey chasing a weasel, whether around a mulberry bush or, in another version, a cobbler's bench, is most entertaining. Both animals can run very fast, but the weasel's long tail might make him easy for the monkey to catch.

Briskly (♩.= 1 beat)

1. All a-round the mul-ber-ry bush the mon-key chased the
2. Ru-fus has the whoop-ing cough, poor Sal-ly has the

mf

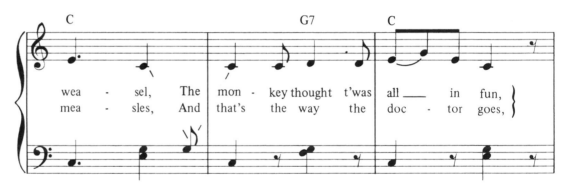

wea - sel, The mon - key thought t'was all ___ in fun,
mea - sles, And that's the way the doc - tor goes,

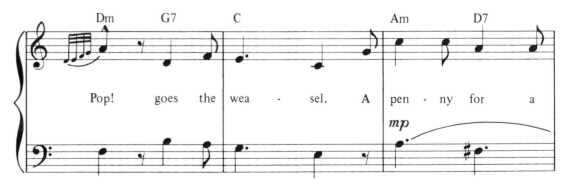

Pop! goes the wea - sel. A pen - ny for a

mp

spool of thread, A pen ny for a nee dle,

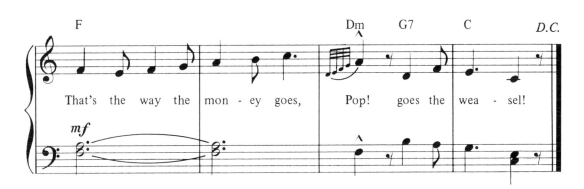

That's the way the mon ey goes, Pop! goes the wea sel!

mf

TOP: *Weasel* (detail)
Kyōsai (Kawanabe Shūsaburo), Japanese,
1831–1889
Handscroll, wash drawing, 17 ft. 3½ in. x 10¾ in.

LEFT: *Three Monkeys* (detail)
Mori Sosen, Japanese, 1747–1821
One of a pair of six-panel screens, color on silk,
panel 41 x 15 in., 1785

75

Red River Valley

The title of this song refers to the Red River that flows through Manitoba in Canada, then between North Dakota and Minnesota. The gentle, wistful melody and words suggest that the young girl's sweetheart is leaving on a long journey. The artist who painted this picture did not indicate its location, but he managed to capture much of the same quality as the song.

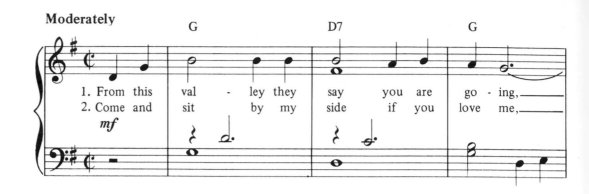

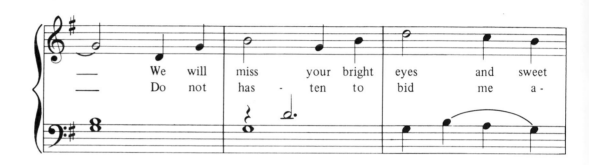

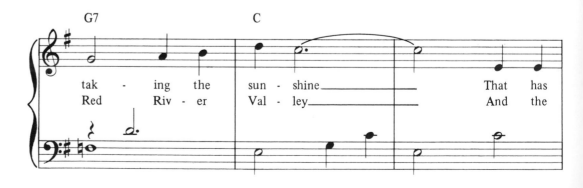

Across the Valley
Gifford Beal, American, 1879–1956
Watercolor and gouache on off-white wove paper,
14⅛ x 20 in., 1916

Scarborough Fair

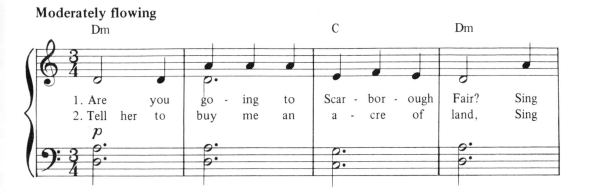

Moderately flowing

Dm ... C ... Dm

1. Are you go - ing to Scar - bor - ough Fair? Sing
2. Tell her to buy me an a - cre of land, Sing

p

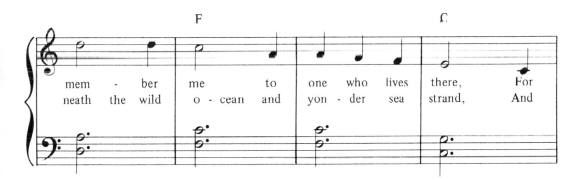

F ... Dm ... F ... G ... Dm

pars - ley, sage, rose - mar - y, and thyme. Re -
pars - ley, sage, rose - mar - y, and thyme, Be -

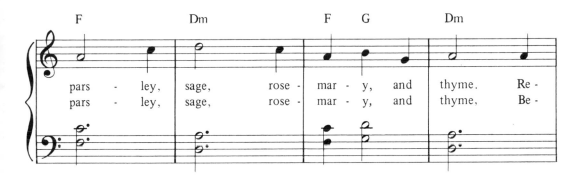

F ... C

mem - ber me to one who lives there, For
neath the wild o - cean and yon - der sea strand, And

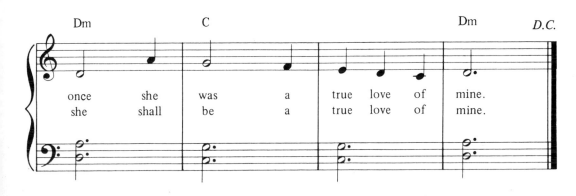

Dm ... C ... Dm ... *D.C.*

once she was a true love of mine.
she shall be a true love of mine.

Beginning in the Middle Ages, yearly fairs were held in Scarborough, England, by royal decree. Fairs were originally held to mark religious holidays, but there was much merrymaking and entertainment at them, too.

Additional verses:

3.

Tell her to make me a cambric shirt,
Sing parsley, sage, rosemary, and thyme,
Without any stitching or needlework,
And she shall be a true love of mine.

4.

Tell her to wash it in yonder dry well,
Sing parsley, sage, rosemary, and thyme,
Where water ne'er sprung nor a drop of
    rain fell,
And she shall be a true love of mine.

5.

Tell her to dry it on yonder sharp thorn,
Sing parsley, sage, rosemary, and thyme,
Which never bore blossom since Adam
    was born,
And she shall be a true love of mine.

The Fair at Bezons (detail)
Jean Baptiste Joseph Pater, French, 1695–1736
Oil on canvas, 42 x 56 in., ca. 1733

She'll Be Comin' 'Round the Mountain

With this spirited, bouncing rhythm, it's easy to picture a small country town where the arrival of the stagecoach was a thing of excitement. People would rush out to greet the coach, to meet long-awaited friends or relatives, to pick up mail, or just to have some fun. This charming color woodcut, by the French artist Lucien Laforge, is an illustration from an alphabet book.

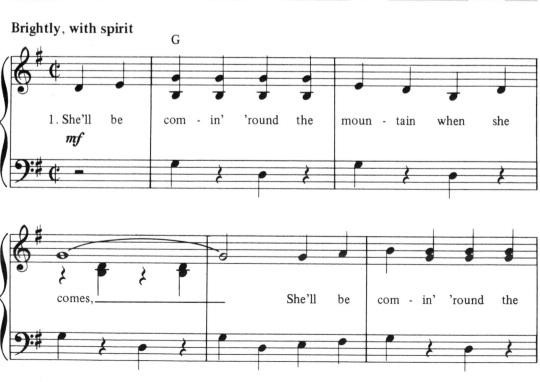

Brightly, with spirit

1. She'll be com - in' 'round the moun - tain when she comes, _____ She'll be com - in' 'round the

mountain when she comes,_____ She'll be

com - in' 'round the moun - tain, she'll be

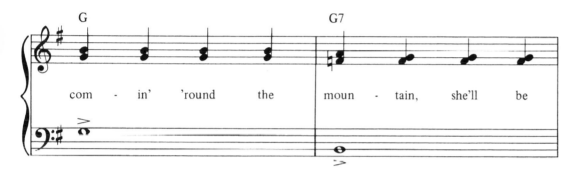

com - in' 'round the moun - tain, She'll be com - in' 'round the

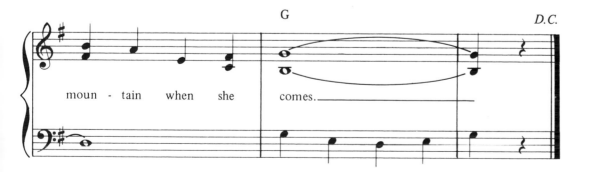

moun - tain when she comes._____

Additional verses:

2.

She'll be drivin' six white horses when
    she comes,
She'll be drivin' six white horses when
    she comes,
She'll be drivin' six white horses,
She'll be drivin' six white horses,
She'll be comin' 'round the mountain
    when she comes.

3.

Oh, we'll all come out to greet her
    when she comes,
Yes, we'll all come out to greet her
    when she comes,
Oh, we'll all come out to greet her,
Yes, we'll all come out to greet her,
She'll be comin' 'round the mountain
    when she comes.

Fantasmagorie (detail)
Lucien Laforge, French, 1889–?
Woodcut from an alphabet series, printed in color,
ca. 1925

Very freely

Shenandoah

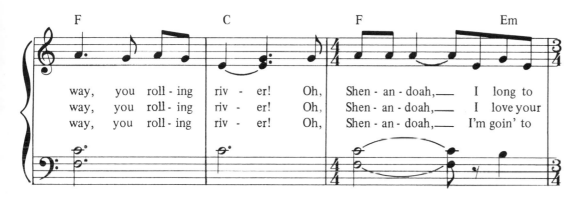

Both the beautiful song "Shenandoah" and George Caleb Bingham's haunting picture *Fur Traders Descending the Missouri* capture the wonder and majesty of America's great rivers. "Shenandoah" is the name of a river and a valley in Virginia, but in the song it becomes a person. The singer's love for Shenandoah's daughter, whom he must leave to cross "the wide Missouri," makes the song all the more romantic.

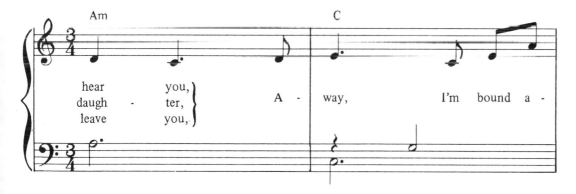

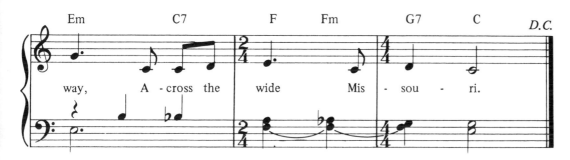

Fur Traders Descending the Missouri
George Caleb Bingham, American, 1811–1879
Oil on canvas, 29 x 36½ in., 1845

Simple Gifts

This is a dancing song that was composed by Joseph Brackett. Brackett was a member of the Shakers, a religious community that thrived in the United States during the eighteenth and nineteenth centuries. The song expresses the belief that to be pure in heart and true to oneself, or "simple" as the Shakers would say, is the greatest gift. The simplicity of the painting at right by the American painter Joshua Johnson captures the essence of the song.

Yellow Basket of Flowers
American, 19th century
Watercolor and gum arabic on off-white wove paper,
15¾ x 19⅝ in.

Moderately

'Tis a gift to be sim-ple, 'tis a gift to be free, 'Tis a

gift to come down to where we ought to be, And

when we find our-selves in the place just right, 'Twill

*Guitar: Capo 3rd fret

be in the val-ley of ____ love and de-light.

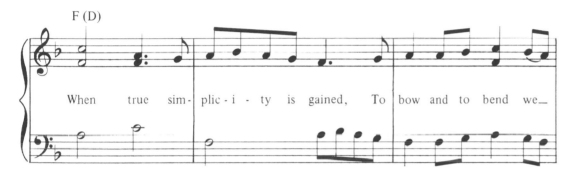

When true sim-plic-i-ty is gained, To bow and to bend we_

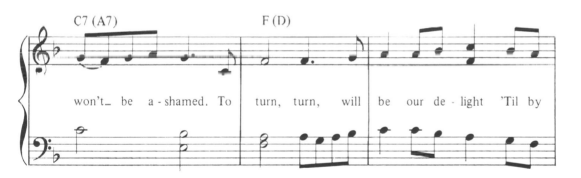

won't_ be a-shamed. To turn, turn, will be our de-light 'Til by

turn-ing and turn-ing we____ come a-round right.

Edward and Sarah Rutter
Joshua Johnson, American, ca. 1763–ca. 1824
Oil on canvas, 36 x 32 in., ca. 1805

Skip to My Lou

There are several traditional dances that are done to the bouncy tune of "Skip to My Lou." In one version, boys and girls choose partners and form a circle. One boy has no partner, and as he moves around the circle and picks a girl, everyone claps and joins in the singing. "Lou" is an old word for sweetheart, and lines like "fly in the buttermilk" give an amusing glimpse of old-fashioned rural life.

May
Franz M. Melchers, Belgian, 1868–1944
Hand-tinted lithograph illustration from *L'An* (poems by Thomas Braun), published in Brussels by E. Lyon-Claesen, 9¹⁵⁄₁₆ x 9¹⁵⁄₁₆ in., 1897

Square-dance tempo

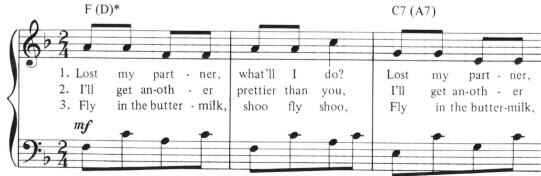

1. Lost my part - ner, what'll I do? Lost my part - ner,
2. I'll get an-oth - er prettier than you, I'll get an-oth - er
3. Fly in the butter - milk, shoo fly shoo, Fly in the butter-milk,

*Guitar: Capo 3rd fret

F (D)

what'll I do? | Lost my part - ner, | what'll I do?
prettier than you, | I'll get an-oth - er | prettier than you,
shoo fly shoo, | Fly in the butter-milk, | shoo fly shoo,

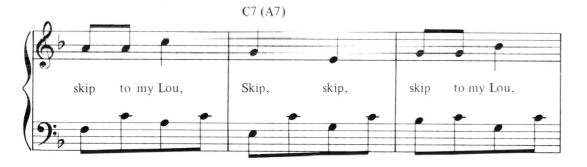

Skip to my Lou, my dar - lin'. | Skip, skip,

C7 (A7)

skip to my Lou, | Skip, skip, | skip to my Lou,

F (D)   C7 (A7)   F (D)
                                                          D.C.

Skip, skip, | skip to my Lou, | Skip to my Lou, my dar - lin'.

Skye Boat Song

This beautiful song recalls a dramatic episode in Scottish history. In 1746, many Highlanders rose in support of the Scotsman Bonnie Prince Charlie as their king, instead of the British king, George II. Prince Charlie was charming and brave, and tried to win back the throne with the aid of Scottish clans, but the Highlanders were crushingly defeated by the British, and Charlie had to escape in an open boat, "over the sea" to the island of Skye.

Purgatory Cliff
William Trost Richards, American, 1833–1905
Watercolor and gouache on light tan wove paper,
13 x 10 in., 1876

Gently, like a boat rocking

Chorus

Speed, bon-ny boat, like a bird on the wing, On-ward, the sail-ors cry!

Car-ry the lad that's born to be king O-ver the sea to Skye.

1. Loud the winds howl! Loud the waves roar! Thun-der clouds rend the air!

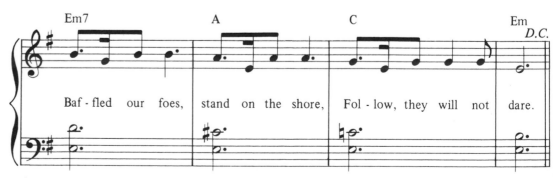

Baf-fled our foes, stand on the shore, Fol-low, they will not dare.

*Last time, end here

2.

Though the waves leap, soft shall ye
    sleep,
Ocean's a royal bed.
Rocked in the deep, Flora will keep
Watch by your weary head.
(Chorus)

3.

Many's the lad fought on that day
Well the claymore could wield.
When the night came, silently lay
Dead on Culloden's field.
(Chorus)

4.

Burn'd are our homes, exile and death
Scatter the loyal men,
Yet, e'er the sword cool in the sheath,
Charlie will come again.
(Chorus)

Sweet Betsy from Pike

This song was a favorite during the Gold Rush in the nineteenth century. Among the hopefuls rushing to seek their fortunes were Sweet Betsy from Pike and her faithful lover, Ike. Like the family in Frederic M. Grant's romantic painting of a stalwart young farmer with his wife and baby, Betsy and Ike have few possessions, but they have each other. With the optimism of youth, they know that there will always be tomorrow.

The Homestead (detail)
Frederic M. Grant, American, 1886–1959
Oil on canvas, 46 x 50½ in., ca. 1930

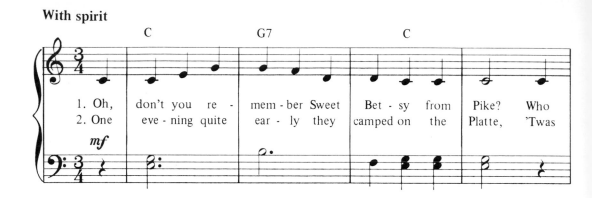

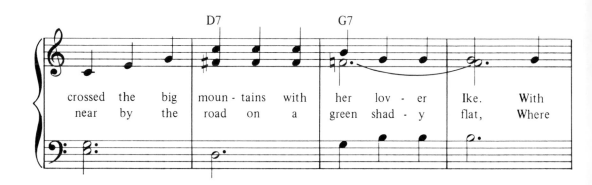

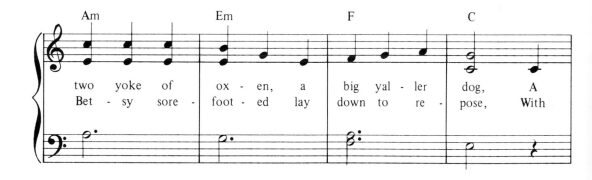

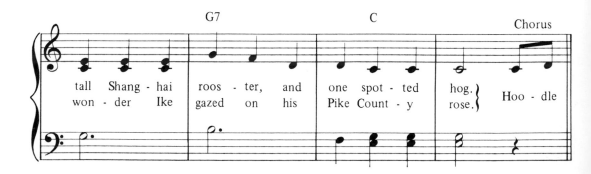

Additional verses:

3.

The Shanghai ran off, and their cattle
    all died.
That morning the last piece of bacon
    was fried.
Poor Ike was discouraged and Betsy
    got mad.
The dog drooped his tail and looked
    wondrously sad.
(Chorus)

4.

They soon reached the desert where
    Betsy gave out,
And down in the sand she lay rolling
    about,
While Ike half distracted looked on
    with surprise,
Saying, "Betsy, get up, you'll get sand
    in your eyes."
(Chorus)

5.

Sweet Betsy got up in a great deal of
    pain,
Declared she'd go back to Pike County
    again;
But Ike gave a sigh, and they fondly
    embraced,
And they traveled along with his arm
    round her waist.
(Chorus)

6.

Repeat first verse and Chorus

There Was an Old Lady

Briskly and rather freely

1. There was an old la-dy who swal-lowed a fly, She swal-lowed a fly, I

In this song the story gets more and more fantastic, and very funny, as the creatures the old lady swallows get bigger and bigger. The woman in this painting looks very prim and serious as she sits holding her white fan, but she obviously likes animals, since she is surrounded by two birds, two butterflies, and a black cat.

don't know why; I hope she don't die. 2. There was an old la-dy who

swal-lowed a spi-der That wrig-gled and wig-gled and jig-gled in-side her. She

swal-lowed the spi-der to catch the fly, She swal-lowed the fly, I

Lady with Her Pets (Molly Wales Fobes) (detail)
Rufus Hathaway, American, 1770—1822
Oil on canvas, 34¼ x 32 in., 1790

92

(continued on page 94)

There Was an Old Lady

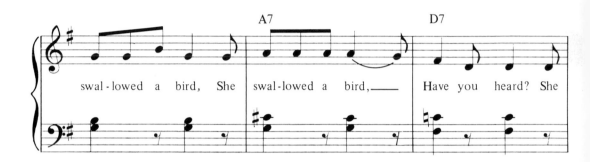

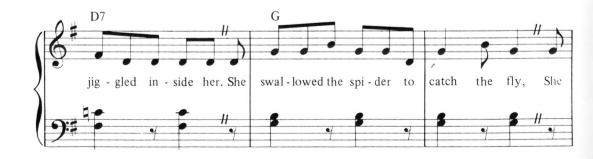

The Cow's Siesta (detail)
Jan Matulka, American, 1890–1972
Watercolor on paper, 24 x 15 in., 1927

swal-lowed the fly, I don't know why; I hope she don't die.

Additional verses:

4.
There was an old lady who swallowed
   a cat,
She swallowed a cat, imagine that!
She swallowed the cat to catch the
   bird,
She swallowed the bird to catch the
   spider, *etc.*

5.
There was an old lady who swallowed
   a dog,
She swallowed a dog as big as a hog.
She swallowed the dog to catch the cat,
She swallowed the cat to catch the
   bird,
She swallowed the bird to catch the
   spider, *etc.*

6.
There was an old lady who swallowed
   a cow,
She swallowed a cow, I don't know
   how.
She swallowed the cow to catch the
   dog,
She swallowed the dog to catch the cat,
She swallowed the cat to catch the
   bird,
She swallowed the bird to catch the
   spider, *etc.*

7.
There was an old lady who swallowed
   a horse ....
(Spoken) She died of course!

Credits

Page 7:
Jacques and Natasha Gelman Collection, 1998   1999.363.3
Photograph by Malcolm Varon
Page 8:
Purchase, Joseph Pulitzer Bequest, 1939   39.108.1
Page 10:
Gift of Colonel Charles A. Fowler, 1921   21.115.3
Page 13:
Catharine Lorillard Wolfe Collection, Bequest of Catharine Lorillard Wolfe, 1887   87.15.77
Page 14:
Gift of Henry Keney Pomeroy, 1927   27.181
Page 17:
Museum Accession
Page 18:
Bequest of Maria DeWitt Jesup, fom the collection of her husband, Morris K. Jesup, 1914   15.30.60
Page 21:
Bequest of Collis P. Huntington, 1900   25.110.5
Page 22:
Gift of the family of Colin Campbell Cooper, in memory of the artist and his wife, 1941   41.22
Page 25:
Gift of Dr. and Mrs. Harold B. Bilsky, 1975   1975.282.1h
Photograph by Bob Hanson
Page 26:
Arthur Hoppock Hearn Fund, 1937   37.60.1
Page 29:
Edward Elliott Family Collection, Purchase, The Dillon Fund Gift, 1981   1981.285.3 g
Page 30:
The Elisha Whittelsey Collection, The Elisha Whittelsey Fund, 1967   67.763.1
Page 33:
Munsey Fund, 1934   34.138
Page 34:
Kathryn E. Hurd Fund, 1995   1995.133
Page 36:
Fletcher Fund, 1937   37.119.1
Page 37:
Bequest of Miss Adelaide Milton de Groot (1876–1967), 1967   67.187.145
Pages 38, 39:
Rogers Fund, 1907   07.123
Photograph by Geoffrey Clements
Page 40:
Gift of Irwin Untermyer, 1964   64.101.1317
Page 43:
Fletcher Fund, 1947   47.18.9
Page 44:
Purchase, Joseph Pulitzer Bequest, 1918   JP 643
Page 47:
The Lesley and Emma Sheafer Collection, Bequest of Emma A. Sheafer, 1973   1974.356.24
Page 48:
The Edward W. C. Arnold Collection of New York Prints, Maps, and Pictures, Bequest of Edward W. C. Arnold, 1954   54.90.159
Photograph by Geoffrey Clements
Page 49:
Edith C. Blum Fund, 1983   1983.122.1
Page 50:
Bequest of Moses Tanenbaum, 1937   39.47.1
Page 51:
TOP: Harris Brisbane Dick Fund, 1929   29.40.8
ABOVE: Museum Accession, 1921   21.36.98

Page 53:
Gift of Mr. and Mrs. Walter C. Crawford, 1967   67.24
Page 54:
The Jules Bache Collection, 1949   49.7.46
Page 57:
Gift of Mr. and Mrs. Paul Bird Jr., 1962   62.696.28
Page 58:
Gift of Mrs. B. J. O. Nordfeldt, 1955   55.634.79
Page 61:
Amelia B. Lazarus Fund, 1910   10.228.3
Page 62:
Bequest of Charles F. Iklé, 1963   64.27.3
Photograph by Geoffrey Clements
Page 63:
Museum Accession
Page 65:
Gift of Dr. and Mrs. Robert E. Carroll, 1982   1982.182.1
Page 66:
Gift of Thomas Kensett, 1874   74.24
Page 68:
Fletcher Fund, 1925   25.97.5
Page 70:
Purchase, Anonymous Gift, 1987   1987.294.4
Page 71:
Purchase, Lila Acheson Wallace Gift, 1988   1988.59
Page 73:
Rogers Fund, 1969   69.182
Page 74:
Charles Stewart Smith Collection, Gift of Mrs. Charles Stewart Smith, Charles Stewart Smith Jr., and Howard Caswell Smith, in memory of Charles Stewart Smith, 1914   14.76.65 e
Page 75:
Fletcher Fund, 1937   37.119.2
Page 77:
Rogers Fund, 1924   24.49.2
Photograph by Geoffrey Clements
Page 78:
The Jules Bache Collection, 1949   49.7.52
Page 80:
Harris Brisbane Dick Fund, 1930   30.96.7
Page 82:
Morris K. Jesup Fund, 1933   33.61
Page 84:
Gift of Edgar William and Bernice Chrysler Garbisch, 1966   66.242.4
Page 85:
Gift of Edgar William and Bernice Chrysler Garbisch, 1965   65.254.3
Photograph by Paul Warchol
Page 86:
The Elisha Whittelsey Collection, The Elisha Whittelsey Fund, 1967   67.763.1
Page 89:
Bequest of Susan Dwight Bliss, 1966   67.55.141
Photograph by Geoffrey Clements
Page 91:
Gift of George D. Pratt, 1933   33.94
Page 93:
Gift of Edgar William and Bernice Chrysler Garbisch, 1963   63.201.1
Page 95:
The Lesley and Emma Sheafer Collection, Bequest of Emma A. Sheafer, 1973   1974.356.14 a